# What Every Teen Needs to Know

Written and Edited by
Douglas Pagels

**Blue Mountain Press**™
Boulder, Colorado

We gratefully acknowledge the permission granted by the following authors, publishers, and authors' representatives to reprint poems or excerpts from their publications: Excerpts from DISNEY'S POOH'S GRAND ADVENTURE: THE SEARCH FOR CHRISTOPHER ROBIN by Kathy Henderson published by Mouse Works are © Disney Enterprises, Inc. and are used by permission. Based on the "Winnie the Pooh" works by A. A. Milne and E. H. Shepard. All rights reserved. Cader Books for "You are a very special person..." by Desmond Tutu, "Achieving your personal best..." by Bonnie Blair, and "You are capable of more..." by Edward O. Wilson from THE MOST IMPORTANT THINGS I KNOW, compiled by Lorne A. Adrain. Copyright © 1997 by Lorne A. Adrain. All rights reserved. HarperCollins Publishers for "One of the most important parts..." and "Your body needs..." from GO FOR THE GOAL by Mia Hamm and Aaron Heifetz. Copyright © 1999 by Mia Hamm. All rights reserved. And for "My daily mission..." and "It wasn't until I was..." from IT'S NOT ABOUT THE BRA by Brandi Chastain. Copyright © 2004 by Brandi Chastain. All rights reserved. And for "Some kids knew that..." from HAWK: OCCUPATION: SKATEBOARDER by Tony Hawk. Copyright © 2001 by Tony Hawk. All rights reserved. And for "I was an eighteen-year-old kid..." and "I've had things to work through..." from CHASING DOWN THE DAWN by Jewel Kilcher. Copyright © 2000 by Jewel Kilcher. All rights reserved. And for "While body type is something..." and "I think actress Kate Winslet..." from TEENAGE FITNESS: GET FIT, LOOK GOOD, AND FEEL GREAT! by Kathy Kaehler. Copyright © 2001 by Kathy Kaehler. All rights reserved. And for "I have lost a lot of friends..." from LADIES FIRST by Queen Latifah and Karen Hunter. Copyright © 1999 by Queen Latifah, Inc. All rights reserved. And for "People removed from addiction..." and "I am learning that..." by Mary Alice Williams and "In terms of what has happened..." by Patricia Neal from QUIET TRIUMPHS by Mary Alice Williams. Copyright © 1999 by Mary Alice Williams. All rights reserved.

Acknowledgments are continued on the last page.

Library of Congress Control Number: 2010900509
ISBN: 978-1-59842-494-2

Printed in China.
First Printing: 2010

♲ This book is printed on recycled paper.

This book is printed on paper that has been specially produced to be acid free (neutral pH) and contains no groundwood or unbleached pulp. It conforms with the requirements of the American National Standards Institute, Inc., so as to ensure that this book will last and be enjoyed by future generations.

# Blue Mountain Arts, Inc.
P.O. Box 4549, Boulder, Colorado 80306

# Contents

(Authors listed in order of first appearance)

# If You Do These Ten Things...
## you will be able to see your way through just about anything

■ Stay positive! (Hopeful people are happier people.) ■ Choose wisely. (Good choices will come back to bless you.) ■ Remember what matters. (The present moment. The good people in it. Hopes and dreams and feelings.)

■ Don't stress out over things you can't control. (Just don't.) ■ Count every blessing. (Even the little ones add up to a lot.) ■ Be good to your body. (It's the only one you get.)

■ Listen to the wishes of your heart. (It always seems to know what's true, what's right, what to do, and where to go with your life.)

■ Understand how special you are! ■ Realize how strong you can be. ■ And know that, YES, you're going to make it through, no matter what.

Maybe you won't be dancing in the streets or jumping on the bed... but you are going to get through the day, the night, and each and every moment that lies ahead. (I promise.)

III Douglas Pagels

I know it's not easy growing up. It never has been, but these days... I think it's harder than ever.

And I just want you to be careful out there in the world... because you mean the whole world to me.

I care about you so much, and no matter what comes along... I hope you'll never forget: you're a strong, smart, and very special person, and I have faith in you to do what is right... for your happiness, your hopes and dreams, your personal well-being, your tomorrows, and your life.

IIIDouglas Pagels

I want everything to work out for you just the way you want it to.

▮▮▮R. L. Keith

Promise me you'll always remember: you're braver than you believe, and stronger than you seem, and smarter than you think.

▮▮▮Christopher Robin to Winnie the Pooh

You are a very special person — become what you are.

▮▮▮Desmond Tutu

# Be Yourself

Hold on to your dreams, and never let them go ■ Show the world how wonderful you are ■ Wish on a star that shines in your sky ■ Rely on all the strength you have inside ■ Stay in touch with those who touch your life with love ■ Look on the bright side, and don't let adversity keep you from winning ■ Be yourself, because you are filled with special qualities that have brought you this far and that will always see you through ■ Keep your spirits up ■ Make your heart happy, and let it reflect on everything you do!

❚❚❚Douglas Pagels

One of the most important parts of being a winner in life is being happy. A happy person makes those around them happy as well, and that is one of the greatest gifts of all. Make decisions in your life that lead to happiness.

⦀Mia Hamm

Your own special horizon is out there now — your goal, your hope, your special wish — just waiting to get a visit from you.

⦀Douglas Pagels

# You Hold the Key

I've got something to say to you, and I hope you will listen with an open heart. Don't be so worried about what everybody else thinks of you, and don't think your happiness depends on someone else.

I want you to just trust yourself. Trust that if you take care of yourself on the inside, follow your instincts, and let yourself evolve naturally, your potential for happiness will be so much greater.

III Trisha Yearwood

This was the turning point for me. I was forced to believe in myself and not in what others thought of me. It was one of the hardest lessons I've ever gone through, and it changed my life forever.

III Alicia Keys

Has anyone told you lately... what a wonderful person you are?

I hope so! I hope you've been told dozens of times... because you are just amazing. And in case you haven't heard those words in a while, I want you to hear them now. You deserve to know that...

It takes someone special to do what you do. It takes someone rare and remarkable to make the lives of everyone around them so much nicer. It takes someone everyone can be proud of... a youthful soul who is learning and growing and going toward the horizons that lie ahead. It takes someone who is living proof of how precious a person can be.

It takes someone... just like you.

III Douglas Pagels

# Words to Help You Be Strong Along the Path of Life

I can barely begin to tell you of all my wishes for you ■ There are so many of them, and I want them all to come true ■ I want you to use your heart as a compass as you grow and find your way in the world, but I want you to always have an appreciation for the direction of home ■ I want you to have self-esteem and self-confidence and be self-sufficient, but also to know that you will never be alone ■ I want you to be safe and smart and cautious ■ I want you to be wise beyond your years ■ I don't want you to grow up too fast ■ I want you to come to me with your fears ■ I want the people who share your days to realize that they are in the presence of a very special someone ■ You are a wonderful, rare person with no comparison ■

I want you to know that opportunities will come, and you'll have many goals to achieve ■ The more that obstacles get in the way of your dreams, the more you'll need to believe ■ Get your feet wet with new experiences, but be sure you never get in over your head ■ I want you to realize how capable you are and that your possibilities are unlimited ■ I hope you never lose your childlike wonder, your appreciation and delight in interesting things ■ I know you'll keep responding in a positive way to the challenges life always brings ■ I want you to set the stage for living in a way that reflects good choices and a great attitude ■ I want you to honor... the wonder of you ■

■■■ Douglas Pagels

# How Will the Value
## of Your Days Be Measured?

What will matter is not what you bought, but what you built; not what you got, but what you gave.

What will matter is not your success, but your significance.

What will matter is every act of integrity, compassion, courage, or sacrifice that enriched, empowered, or encouraged others.

What will matter is not your competence, but your character.

What will matter is not how many people you knew, but how many people felt good when they were around you.

What will matter is how you will be remembered, by whom, and for what.

Living a life that matters doesn't happen by accident. It's not a matter of circumstance, but of choice.

Choose to live a life that matters.

**|||** Anonymous

As a young man I learned a very valuable lesson: I have a choice. Every morning when I wake up I have a choice in how I want to spend my day. I have a choice in how I want to feel, how I treat people, and what my disposition will be. For most of my life I have been very positive. It's just easier.

**▌▌**Rocky Blier

Don't be pushed by your problems.
Be led by your dreams.

**▌▌**Anonymous

Make choices that keep the peace and make you feel proud of how you represent yourself.

III Venus Williams

My daily mission is to... become a better decision maker.

III Brandi Chastain

Whatever good you put out in the universe [will] come back, and whatever bad you put out [will] come back as well.

III Oprah Winfrey

# It's Pretty Much Up to You!

Decisions are incredibly important things! Good decisions will come back to bless you. Bad decisions can come back to haunt you.

That's why it's so important that you take the time to choose wisely. Choose to do the things that reflect well... on your ability, your integrity, your spirit, your health, your tomorrows, your smiles, your dreams, and yourself.

You are such a wonder. You're the only one in the universe exactly like you! I want you to take care of that rare and remarkable soul. I want you to know that there is someone who will thank you for doing the things you do now with foresight and wisdom and respect. It's the person you will someday be.

You have a chance to make that person so thankful and so proud. All you have to do is remember one of the lessons I learned when I made a similar journey. It's pretty simple, really; just these eight words:

Each time you're given the chance... choose wisely.

⦀ Douglas Pagels

# Teens Have It Tough

There was social pressure at [my high school], but my mother and I couldn't begin to keep up with the Joneses, so we didn't even try....

I felt shunned at times. I was the guy who did weird sports and who didn't wear the right labels.

❙❙❙Lance Armstrong

Don't let life discourage you; everyone who got where he is had to begin where he was.

❙❙❙R. L. Evans

Some kids knew that "Tony Hawk" was a professional skater who lived in the area because a local news program had aired a story on me. But nobody connected the featured skater to their skinny classmate.

### ▌▌▌

Doing your own thing during elementary school is one thing; nobody's going to really hassle you. But once you hit the big leagues of high school, it's a whole different ball game....

You should have seen me in the seventh grade when I was growing! Birds could have used me for nesting material. Muscle tone was something I'd only read about. I was also so short, I could have shopped in Baby Gap....

I was the smallest kid in school. It was considered a high school, but it included eighth and ninth graders. I barely looked old enough to be in the eighth grade. I was a bottom feeder.

I could no longer employ the crying plan that had worked so efficiently in preschool (don't think I didn't give it some serious thought), so I tried to recede into the walls. If someone had sold school camouflage, I'd have been his best customer.

▌▌▌ Tony Hawk

So much has happened since *American Idol*.... [I] wanted to share stories about my life in the hope that it might enable a handful of other people to feel better about themselves.

I was dubbed a loser throughout most of my childhood. As a kid, I was an insult magnet — a nerd who loved his grandparents, who wore the wrong clothes, who liked the wrong things, who had goofy hair and glasses, who didn't smoke or drink.

It made for a lonely childhood. More than a decade later, I figured out that the real reason people didn't like me was that *I* didn't like me. When I learned to believe in myself, to have faith and to remain stubborn in my convictions, my life changed. Once I decided I was okay, other people agreed. And those folks who didn't agree didn't matter so much anymore....

By senior year, I was just as popular as anybody else... I had gone from being school bottom-feeder to being one of the most well-liked students in school. It was surreal.

My recognition had nothing to do with anything external. My mama still wouldn't buy me nice clothes. I still had big old glasses and hair that nothing could be done with... I was still skinny and uncoordinated.

The only thing different about me was how I felt about myself.

**III** Clay Aiken

I needed to realize that being different is not always a bad thing, that it can be a good thing as well. That helped me figure out who I was, and who I wanted to be. Even now, my friends make fun of me, tell me, "You're different, Chamique," and they're not just talking about basketball. They say I'm old-fashioned. They're right. What I know, though, is that being old-fashioned may be different, but there's nothing wrong with that. I'm proud of the way I am.

In high school I'd go to dances and social events, but even then I wasn't really into it. I think maybe I went to two parties my whole high school career. I didn't fit in in those situations, but I didn't really care... I just kept it real.

■■■ Chamique Holdsclaw

I was an eighteen-year-old kid with creativity, talent, and potential. I was also an eighteen-year-old kid who was insecure, highly self-critical, and prone to dark moods of doubt and depression....

The thing I have had to work on most diligently is correcting these negative tendencies because if they go unchecked they can run rampant. I have had to work hard and stay constantly focused — why am I so hard on myself... why do I doubt so often... why am I sad?...

Through the years, I have regained myself. I have also learned to access that miraculous center I lived in so instinctively as a child. It has never been lost. It was only buried. My light wasn't damaged or broken. It was wrapped in layers of doubt and insecurity. Somehow, just knowing that seemed to help a lot. Now it's just a question of remembering what's inside me and acting on it, day by day.

**III** Jewel

I was always looking outside myself for strength and confidence, but it comes from within. It was there all the time.

**I I I** Anna Freud

I hope the person I'm becoming won't forget how it felt to be the person I am.

**I I I** Anonymous

I am aware that I am less than some people prefer me to be, but most people are unaware that I am so much more than what they see.

**I I I** Douglas Pagels

# Don't Post *That* Picture

In this day and age, just about everyone is on social networking sites, sharing more about their private lives than ever before. Sharing, connecting, and communicating on the Internet are like a lot of things. There's a really good side... and there's a really bad side. The side that can suddenly change everything for the worse can rear its ugly head if you don't understand the consequences of posting personal pictures and information. The rule of thumb should be this: if you wouldn't want your parents, teachers, or grandparents to see it or read it, don't post it.

You may think you're only sharing that embarrassing story with your friends, but you're not. And if you have the impression that the cell phone picture you're thinking of sending to just one special person will stop there, you're being too naive... and gambling with way too much. When a regrettable picture winds up online, it can be there forever... for anyone in the world to see. It can shadow you throughout your entire life. It can affect future plans, schools, jobs, and relationships. That's a sad truth and a sorry situation. But there is a solution to the problem: just don't do it to begin with. It's as easy, as rewarding, and as reassuring as that.

❚❚❚ Douglas Pagels

People... can constantly put you in an uncomfortable and vulnerable position. I learned this the hard way. By the time I found the courage to voice my feelings, a magazine was already on the newsstands, on *every* corner, with a photograph that embarrassed me, and I had to live with it. There was nothing I could do about it. It was devastating to me because it presented me in a light that I didn't want to stand in and worse, I hadn't felt comfortable with the photo shoot all along. I just didn't know how to say no to them because I was inexperienced. So I doubted myself, but in my gut I knew the whole time that it wasn't right.

Long after, in my mind, I tried to find reasons to justify it, but the only justification I could come up with was that this was something that showed me how strong I would have to be to stand up for what I believe to be true, no matter what some fool thinks. That fool doesn't have to sleep with my conscience every night.

||| Alicia Keys

When you cut corners with what you know is right, you're risking your good name, your reputation.

▋▋▋ Maria Shriver

Watch your thoughts; they become words. Watch your words; they become actions. Watch your actions; they become your habits. Watch your habits; they become character. Watch your character, for it becomes your destiny.

▋▋▋ Anonymous

Character is made by what you stand for; reputation by what you fall for.

▋▋▋ Robert Quillen

# Stand for Something, or You'll Fall for Anything

I wanted everybody to love *me* so badly that for years I let other people's plans and priorities run my life. I allowed others to take from me without giving back, to goad or guilt me into solving their problems, to use me for their own ends, all because I was scared of losing their love and approval....

People who *really* love you don't put conditions on their feelings. They don't say, "I'll love you as long as you do what I want you to." Or, "I'll love you on the condition you continue to please me." They say, "I love you" — period, end of sentence.

Since I reached this understanding, it's impossible to overstate how different my life is. How much richer and fuller and *easier*. While I'm not insensitive to the needs and wants of others, I have learned how crucial it is to honor my own.

||| Patti LaBelle

Not using good judgment in choosing your friends and hanging out with the wrong crowd can undermine all the good things you've done and great decisions you've made.

||| Serena Williams

You don't need a certain number of friends, only a number of friends you can be certain of.

||| Anonymous

Don't hang out with anyone who doesn't understand why you're so wonderful, or who needs to be told, or who doesn't tell you at regular intervals when you forget.

||| Lisa Scottoline

# Social... Security

Some of the luckiest people in the world are those who have a wonderful friend to share life with...

A friend who cares and who shares the gifts of smiles and closeness and companionship. Someone with whom you have so much in common. Somebody who's a precious part of the best memories you'll ever make. A special friend. A true friend. One to confide in, one who never lets you down, and one who always understands. A friend who is simply amazing because their heart is so big, their soul is so beautiful, and because everything about them inspires everything that is good about you.

III Douglas Pagels

# Checking Out That Person in the Mirror

You are something — and someone — very special. You really are. No one else in this entire world is exactly like you, and there are so many incredible things about you.

You're a one-of-a-kind treasure, uniquely here in this space and time. You are here to shine in your own wonderful way, sharing your smile in the best way you can, and remembering all the while that a little light somewhere makes a brighter light everywhere. You can — and you do — make a wonderful contribution to this world.

You have qualities within you that many people would love to have, and those who really and truly know you... are so glad that they do. You have a big heart and a good and sensitive soul. You are gifted with thoughts and ways of seeing things that only special people know.

You know that life doesn't always play by the rules, but that in the long run, everything will work out.

You understand that you and your actions are capable of turning anything around — and that joys once lost can always be found. There is a resolve and an inner reserve of strength in you that few ever get to see. You have so many treasures within — those you're only beginning to discover and all the ones you're already aware of.

Never forget what a treasure you are. That special person in the mirror may not always get to hear all the compliments you so sweetly deserve, but you are so worthy of such an abundance...

of friendship, joy, and love.

❙❙❙ Douglas Pagels

# Thirteen Things
# I Don't Want You to Do

Don't ~ stress out about things you have no control
over. Sometimes what is... just is.

Don't ~ waste your days in emotional disarray over a
negative situation that you *can* be in control of.
(Remember, you always have *at least* three options:
move on, stay where you are and just deal with it, or
turn a negative situation into a positive one.)

Don't ~ try to fit in with the "right" crowd when it feels
too forced. The best friendships are the ones that are
natural and easy and comfortable and kind. Find
one of those.

Don't ~ be a part of prejudice against anyone. Be
colorblind and open-minded to the millions who
have diverse beliefs and varying backgrounds.

Don't ~ worry about your future. It will unfold slowly
enough and give you plenty of time to help you
decide... all the wheres and whens and whys.

Don't ~ feel like you have to put up with people who
are rude or obnoxious. Always take the higher
ground when you can, but if you need a release, take
comfort in quietly thinking to yourself, "I'm really
glad I'm not you..." and leave it at that.

Don't ~ forget, though, that some people have emotional
or physical things going on beneath the surface, and
if we knew what they were, we'd cut them a lot
more slack.

Don't ~ ever forget that reckless behavior and cars are
a deadly mix. People forget that every year, and
when they do, it's often the last thing they'll
ever forget.

Don't ~ be afraid to ask for advice. There are people
who love you and care about you and would like to
help you in any way they can. Be brave... and ask.

Don't ~ be obsessive about your body and your looks.
You're growing and changing, and you are a work in
progress and a miracle in the making. The simple
truth in the looks department is — some people are
always going to seem better and others will always
seem worse. It's okay. We're all different. That's
pretty much the way the world works.

Don't ~ stop there; it's the same with money. There
are the have-nots, the have-a-lots, and everybody
in between. When your perspective gets lost
and you're fretting about not having something
"everyone else" has, remember, some can't afford
the cost of anything.

Don't ~ let cynical people transfer their cynicism off
on you. In spite of all its problems, it is still a pretty
amazing world and there are lots of truly wonderful
people spinning around on this planet.

And don't ~ ever forget: the teen years can definitely
be challenging, but if you work it right... they're
also some of the most memorable and most fun and
most amazing times of life.

❚❚❚ Douglas Pagels

# It's Amazing What Having a Healthy Point of View Can Do

Take care of yourself. Good health is everyone's major source of wealth.

**III** Anonymous

While body type is something you're born with and can't necessarily change, you can change your eating habits and up your level of physical activity.... Never forget that you can firm, tone, define, and enhance what you already have through fitness. Fitness is always a positive way of dealing with everything. It also provides a great release from the mental and emotional frustrations that come with being a teen.

**III** Kathy Kaehler

I developed my escape routines like everybody else.... At the age of fourteen — I would head off alone to places where the steep hills came right down near the road. I climbed dusty trails and boulder-filled avalanche chutes up to the high places. The cool mountain air was a blessed contrast to the overheated atmosphere of home. I would propel my body upward, making a mental pact with myself that if I could just get to the top of the ridge or the peak, all the anxiety that consumed me would fall away. It usually worked, too. Arriving at the top, with my lungs and thighs burning, I would look out and feel things start to sort themselves out, fall into perspective.

||| Mariel Hemingway

I think actress Kate Winslet... has one of the best attitudes in Hollywood when it comes to fitness.

"I am who I am," she says. "I'm healthy. I swim a mile every day. I'll never be a stick insect, and I wouldn't want to be either, because it seems to me that a lot of people who are very thin are just really unhappy.

"I had a time in my life when I was about nineteen and I was very thin, and I wasn't eating. I was anorexic for about six months, and I was so unhappy....

"I feel for those people [anorexics] because they're being screwed up by what is said to be beautiful and successful these days, thin and pretty, and it's just 'a crock.'

"Because of the person I am, I won't be knocked down — ever. They can do what they like," she says. "They can say I'm fat, I'm thin, I'm whatever, and I'll never stop. I just won't. I've got too much to do. I've too much to be happy about."

III Kathy Kaehler

When I became a teenager, I experienced times when I felt insecure about my looks. I wished that my face were more attractive... and wished that I were slimmer....

During those years there were many times I wished that I could mix and match body parts with someone else.... Over time, my physical features all caught up with one another and everything balanced out. As that happened, I started to come into my own and grow comfortable in my skin. At some point it just dawned on me that this is the body God gave me and I love and appreciate it no matter what.

▌▌▌ Serena Williams

It wasn't until I was a freshman in college that I got comfortable with my body....

I came to understand that this is who I am, and this is what I'm working with, as the expression goes, and I'm comfortable with myself.

▌▌▌ Brandi Chastain

Your body needs every edge it can get.... That means eating good foods... and of course, avoiding drugs, alcohol, and cigarettes.

**|||** Mia Hamm

I don't like to abuse alcohol — anything you abuse will abuse you back.

**|||** Bono

Being surrounded by smokers and drinkers was a recipe for disaster.

**|||** Lynn Marie Smith

I got sucked into the world of dancing, raving, and even bragging about how many clubs and pills I consumed each weekend (which seemed to be extending each week). My moods were uncontrollable. I went from feeling great one second to wanting to rip my own skin off the next. I was pushing away my friends, family, and pushing myself into an extremely dark and lonely place....

It was the most hellish nightmare that you could imagine and I was living it... My own self-made hell.

I could go on and on, but for two weeks I had to be in a psychiatric ward where I was scared, heavily medicated, and praying to God to get me out of the huge mess that I had made for myself....

I guess the whole point of me writing this to you is that if I can change the mind of one person to think twice before using... any drug... I will feel a little more complete. You never think it can happen to you until it does.

▌▌▌Lynn Marie Smith
(featured on the MTV show *True Life*)

# Avoid Wrong Turns
# and Dangerous Detours

I have lost a lot of friends... they became addicted to various substances. They could never feel how far was too far. They thought that they could handle anything, stay in control of the substances that were making them feel invincible, that were egging them on to cross any boundary....

We always have an "it won't happen to me" attitude when we see other people making mistakes. Don't be fooled. It can happen to you — if you aren't careful, if you don't know who you are — anything can happen.

III Queen Latifah

People removed from addiction often say, why don't they just quit? They should just find a way to just say no. Experts in the recovery field tell me that it doesn't work that way. Sure, picking up that first drink, doing that first line, is a personal choice. But few of those who choose to use have any notion of the potential consequences. They have no idea that they are playing Russian roulette. According to statistics, ten percent of them will become addicts; they will ultimately have no choice but to continue using....

It is important to note that in the end, alcohol and drug addictions don't come in bottles, they come in people.

||| Mary Alice Williams

If you ignore what you *know* to be the difference between right and wrong, you'll pay a huge price. And I'm not just talking about losing sleep.

||| Maria Shriver

Each day is a blank page in the diary of your life. And there is something special you need to remember in order to turn your life story into the treasure it deserves to be.

This is how it works...

Follow your dreams. Work hard. Be kind. This is all anyone could ever ask: do what you can to make the door open on a day that is filled with inspiration in some special way.

Remember: Goodness will be rewarded. Smiles will pay you back. Have fun. Find strength. Be truthful. Have faith. Don't focus on anything you lack.

Realize that people are the treasures in life, and happiness is the real wealth. Have a diary that describes how you are doing your best, and...

The rest will take care of itself.

▮▮▮ Douglas Pagels

Achieving your personal best is all one can ask of themselves. If the results are first, fourth, or thirtieth, and it is the best you have ever done, then that is something to be proud of.

■■■ Bonnie Blair

You are capable of more than you know. Choose a goal that seems right for you and strive to be the best, however hard the path. Aim high... Persist! The world needs all you can give.

■■■ Edward O. Wilson

# Twenty-Four Things to Always Remember... and One Thing to Never Forget

Your presence is a present to the world.
You're unique and one of a kind.
Your life can be what you want it to be.
Take the days just one at a time.

Count your blessings, not your troubles.
You'll make it through whatever comes along.
Within you are so many answers.
Understand, have courage, be strong.

Don't put limits on yourself.
So many dreams are waiting to be realized.
Decisions are too important to leave to chance.
Reach for your peak, your goal, your prize.

Nothing wastes more energy than worrying.
The longer one carries a problem, the heavier it gets.
Don't take things too seriously.
Live a life of serenity, not a life of regrets.

Remember that a little love goes a long way.
Remember that a lot... goes forever.
Remember that friendship is a wise investment.
Life's treasures are people... together.

Realize that it's never too late.
Do ordinary things in an extraordinary way.
Have health and hope and happiness.
Take the time to wish upon a star.

And don't ever forget...
     for even a day... how very special you are.

❚❚❚ Douglas Pagels

# Hitting the Books

Serena and I believe there's nothing more important in life than getting a good education. We want you to become so determined to learn that you don't allow anyone or anything to come between you and your schoolwork....

The people and conditions in your life change from day to day. But the things you learn will always stay with you. Knowledge is the one thing that no one can take away from you — ever, no matter what. This is really important for you to understand.... The more you learn, the better your future will be and the more choices you'll have.

||| Venus Williams

I feel like there are a lot of different things that can educate you in life.

||| Taylor Swift

Get... involved in as many activities as possible. Try everything: sports, music, art... choir... drama.... You never know where you're going to find your niche. I found mine, and it changed my life.

||| Picabo Street

I truly believe that knowledge is the key to being successful in life. Thus, I feel it is necessary for you to put your best effort into your studies and all of your assignments! If you make a habit to do that now, when you go on to college and your first job, life will be that much easier!

||| Connie Chung

# When Times Are Tough...
## I know you'll make it through,
### because I know these things about you

In the days ahead, I know you will stay as
strong as you need to be... to see your way
through anything that comes along. I know
you will discover more courage and hope and
faith inside you than you even knew you had.

I know things will get better, day by day, and
that the passage of time has a wonderful way
of helping you see things in the right light. And
I know you can do every positive thing it takes
to make it through any difficult time, because...
that's what remarkable people do. And one of
those very special people, without a doubt...
will always be you.

▌▌▌ Douglas Pagels

I've had things to work through, and sorrows, but I can say to others who have suffered that we are whole no matter how broken we feel, and we can recover the experience of our wholeness, no matter our age.

||| Jewel

There are two ways to react to bad things. The easy way is to get angry, cast aspersions, and generally get in a bad mood about the world and everything in it.... The other way to react takes a lot more work. You can get over it. That's right; accept it, be happy you survived it, and get past it....

We are often at our best when we're facing our worst situations. Know that when you come out of it, you can be a better you.

||| Kermit the Frog

Always know in your heart that you are far bigger than anything that can happen to you.

**|||** Anonymous

I am learning that while you can't decide what happens to you, you can decide what happens in you.

**|||** Mary Alice Williams

In terms of what has happened in my life, I don't quite understand it. I don't know why some people are picked on and some people aren't. But you just can't be a sissy. You can't give up.... I'm just going to continue to do the best in this life.

**|||** Patricia Neal

# I Wish for You

Happiness. Deep down within.
Serenity. With each sunrise.
Success. In each facet of your life.
Close and caring friends.
Love. That never ends.

Special memories. Of all
  the yesterdays.
A bright today. With so much
  to be thankful for.
A path. That leads to
  beautiful tomorrows.

Dreams. That do their best to come true.
And appreciation. Of all the wonderful
  things about you.

▮▮▮ Douglas Pagels

# Things That Are Going to Happen in Your Life...
## (if they haven't already)

- You will be concerned about your future, wonder what's to come, and be uncertain how you'll manage.

- You will manage. As a matter of fact, you'll succeed.

- You will have friendships you will treasure forever.

- You will experience life's immense joys and deep sorrows.

- You will make memories you wouldn't trade for anything.

- You will have times you'd just as soon forget.

- You will be in difficult situations, in places you'd rather not be, or with others who jeopardize your well-being.

■ You will come out of it just fine, as long as you do whatever it takes to get yourself into a better place and put control of the situation into your own hands, not at the whim of someone else.

■ You will eventually, proudly, happily discover that all the good things you can do — having the right attitude, having a strong belief in your abilities, making good choices and responsible decisions — all those good things you can do will pay huge dividends.

■ You'll see. Your prayers will be heard.

■ Your karma will kick in.

■ The sacrifices you made will be repaid.

■ And the good work will have all been worth it.

III Douglas Pagels

# This Is a Time of Wonderful Possibilities

New journeys await you. Decisions lie ahead, wondering... What will you do? Where will you go? How will you choose when the choices are yours?

Remember that good decisions come back to bless you, over and over again. Work for the ability to choose wisely, to prosper, to succeed. Listen with your heart as well as your head to the glimmers of truth that provide advice and inspiration to the hours of your days. And let those truths take you to beautiful places.

Touch the sky, and in your reach,
believe, achieve, and aspire.

I hope your tomorrows take you to the summit of your goals and that your joys take you even higher.

▌▌▌ Douglas Pagels

I sometimes feel like a late bloomer. I feel it would have been possible to do much more, much sooner, if I hadn't been so worried. What I know now... is that there's no time to waste. It's time to be bold about who you really are.

III Ann Curry

I believe that you tend to create your own blessings. You have to prepare yourself so that when opportunity comes, you're ready.

III Oprah Winfrey

And when you get the choice to watch on the sidelines or to dance, get out there and dance.

III Lee Ann Womack

# Acknowledgments continued…

We gratefully acknowledge the permission granted by the following authors, publishers, and authors' representatives to reprint poems or excerpts from their publications: Broadway Books, a division of Random House, Inc., and The Creative Culture, Inc., for "I've got something to say…" by Trisha Yearwood, "Don't hang out with anyone who…" by Lisa Scottoline, "I sometimes feel like…" by Ann Curry, and "And when you get the choice…" by Lee Ann Womack from WHAT I KNOW NOW: LETTERS TO MY YOUNGER SELF, edited by Ellyn Spragins. Copyright © 2006 by Ellyn Spragins. Afterword copyright © 2008 by Elly▸ Spragins. All rights reserved. G. P. Putnam's Sons, a division of Penguin Group (USA), Inc., for "This was the turning point for me…" and "People in this business can…" from TEARS FOR WATER: SONGBOOK OF POEMS AND LYRICS by Alicia Keys. Copyright © 2004 by Lellow Brands, Inc. All rights reserved. And for "There was social pressure…" from IT'S NOT ABOUT THE BIKE by Lance Armstrong. Copyright © 2000 by Lance Armstrong. All rights reserved. Fireside, a division of Simon & Schuster, Inc., for "As a young man I learned…" by Rocky Blier from 100 WAYS TO BEAT THE BLUES by Tanya Tucker and Friends. Copyright © 2005 by Tanya Tucker. All rights reserved. Houghton Mifflin Harcourt Publishing Company for "Make choices that keep…," "Not using good judgment…," "When I became a teenager…," and "Serena and I believe there's nothing…" from SERVING FROM THE HIP: 10 RULES FOR LIVING, LOVING, AND WINNING by Venus Williams and Serena Williams. Text copyright © 2005 by Venus Williams and Serena Williams. Reprinted by permission. All rights reserved. John Wiley & Sons, Inc., for "Whatever good you put out…" and "I believe that you tend…" by Oprah Winfrey from OPRAH WINFREY SPEAKS by Janet Lowe. Copyright © 1998 by Janet Lowe. All rights reserved. Random House, Inc., for "So much has happened since…" from LEARNING TO SING by Clay Aiken and Allison Glock. Copyright © 2004 by Clay Aiken. All rights reserved. Aladdin Paperbacks, an imprint of Simon & Schuster Children's Division, for "I needed to realize that…" from CHAMIQUE HOLDSCLAW: MY STORY by Chamique Holdsclaw with Jennifer Frey. Copyright © 2001 by Chamique Holdsclaw. All rights reserved. Grand Central Publishing for "When you cut corners…" and "If you ignore what you…" from TEN THINGS I WISH I'D KNOWN BEFORE I WENT OUT INTO THE REAL WORLD by Maria Shriver. Copyright © 2000 by Maria Shriver. Reprinted by permission of Grand Central Publishing. All rights reserved. And for "I wanted everybody to love *me*…" from PATTI'S PEARLS by Patti LaBelle. Copyright © 2001 by Patti LaBelle and Laura Randolph Lancaster. Reprinted by permission of Grand Central Publishing. All rights reserved. Simon & Schuster, Inc., for "I developed my escape routines…" from FINDING MY BALANCE by Mariel Hemingway. Copyright © 2003 by Fox Creek Productions f/s/o Mariel Hemingway. All rights reserved. Riverhead Books, a division of Penguin Group (USA), Inc., for "I don't like to abuse alcohol…" by Bono from BONO IN CONVERSATIONS WITH MICHKA ASSAYAS by Michka Assayas. Copyright © 2005 by M. Assayas. All rights reserved. Atria Books, a division of Simon & Schuster, Inc., for "Being surrounded by smokers…" and "I got sucked into the world…" from ROLLING AWAY: MY AGONY WITH ECSTASY by Lynn Marie Smith. Copyright © 2005 by Lynn Marie Smith. All▸ rights reserved. The writers of *Whirl Magazine*, www.whirlmagazine.com, for "I feel like there are…" by Taylor Swift from "Hi, this is Taylor Swift calling…" (*Whirl*: November 12, 2009). Copyright © 2009 by *Whirl Magazine*. All rights reserved. The McGraw-Hill Companies for "Get… involved in as many…" from▸ PICABO: NOTHING TO HIDE by Picabo Street. Copyright © 2002 by Picabo Street. All rights reserved. Anova Books for "I truly believe that…" by Connie Chung from THE MOST IMPORTANT LESSONS IN LIFE: LETTERS TO A YOUNG GIRL by Rachel Chandler. Copyright © 1998 by Rachel Chandler. All rights reserved. Excerpts from BEFORE YOU LEAP: A FROG'S EYE VIEW OF LIFE'S GREATEST LESSONS by Kermit the Frog published by Disney are © The Muppets Studio LLC and are used by permission. All rights reserved.

A careful effort has been made to trace the ownership of selections used in this anthology in order to obtain permission to reprint copyrighted material and give proper credit to the copyright owners. If any error or omission has occurred, it is completely inadvertent, and we would like to make corrections in future editions provided that written notification is made to the publisher:

BLUE MOUNTAIN ARTS, INC., P.O. Box 4549, Boulder, Colorado 80306.